The Boomtastic A-Z of Jokes

BASIL BRUSH™

Joketionary

This is a Carlton book

First published by in Great Britain by Carlton Books Limited 2004
20 Mortimer Street
London W1T 3JW

AUTHOR: ROD GREEN

Text and design copyright © Carlton Books Ltd 2004

ISBN 1 84442 661 0

Printed and bound in Great Britain

The Boomtastic A-Z of Jokes

BASIL BRUSH™

Joketionary

CARLTON
BOOKS

4 Boomtastic

Oi, moosh!

Feeling a bit **down** in the DUMPS?
Feeling MOPEY, MOANY, MUGGY and
MUDDLED? Has Captain Coldheart sent you the

collywobbles?

Then this is just the thing you need to get the
corners of your mouth pointing back towards
your ears again! This is my BOOMING
MARVELLOUS A to Z of jokes.
It's a positive treasure trove of ticklish
humour, a gigantic gallery of
giggles, a huge HOARD OF
HILARITY.

Like **ALL** good books mine starts at the beginning and finishes at the end, and like **ALL** good dictionaries, it starts at the beginning of the alphabet with A. So the first jokes you'll find in my book are about things beginning with A, like **Aardvark** and, let me assure you, finding a joke with Aardvark in it wasn't easy... it was really *ard vark!*

There are oooooodles of jokes ooooozing off these pages and it took me booming ages to find them all. There are cute jokes, CORNY jokes, daft jokes, clever jokes, l o n g jokes and SHORT jokes in this SIDE-SPLITTING, RIB TICKLING collection.

Whether they are long or short, and I like to think the best things in life are a bit on the short side, the entire A to Z of jokes in my *Joketionary* are guaranteed to be...

absolutely

Booming Marvellous

☆ ☆ ☆ ☆ ☆ ☆ ☆ ☆ ☆ ☆ ☆ ☆ ☆ ☆

Aardvark

In the jungle in South America, an explorer was leading his son along an overgrown path when a SMALL AARDVARK stepped out in front of them. "There's nothing to be afraid of," said the explorer to his son. "A little aardvark never hurt anyone..."

Aerial

Two television aerials got married one day. The wedding ceremony was NAFF but the reception was brilliant!

Aliens

Where do aliens park their space ships?

At parking meteors.

What do you do if you see a spaceman?

PARK IN IT, MAN.

Ant

What kind of ants totally spoil your picnic when they run all over the cakes?

Elephants!

Ape

Where do baby apes sleep?

In apricots.

Apple

"Now," said the teacher, "who can tell me who the first woman in the world was? How about you, Helen?" "No, miss," said Helen, it wasn't me. "I know that!" cried the teacher. "I want you to tell me who it was. The woman lived a long time ago. Think of the apple..."

"GRANNY SMITH?"

Architect

What did the French architect call the building he designed from sponge cake, jelly, cream, custard and fruit?

The Trifle Tower!

Ark

Why were the elephants last to board Noah's Ark?

They had to **pack their trunks.**

Arithmetic

There are 3 kinds of people in the world those who CAN COUNT and those who CAN'T.

Armada

What did Sir Francis Drake get out of the Spanish Armada?

About 10 miles to the galleon!

Artist

Which French artist had two toilets?

Two-loos Lautrec

Astronaut

What game do astronauts most like to play?

Moon-opoly!

Atoms

Two atoms **bashed** into each other.

"Oh, no! I've lost an electron!" wailed one.

"Are you sure?" asked the other.

"YES," said the first,

 "I'm positive."

Aunt

Why did batty AUNT NORA keep nutty UNCLE NORMAN under the bed?

She thought he was a *little potty*!

Ball

Why was Cinderella useless at tennis?

She kept running away from the ball.

Cinderella could have been much better at tennis but her COACH was a PUMPKIN!

Banana

BANANAS are never lonely because they

hang around in bunches!

Bank

A man went into his **bank** and said to the bank teller, "I'd like to check my balance, please."

"Of course," said the teller. "Can you stand on ONE LEG on this BEACH BALL"?

Barbecue

Two fish were cooking on a barbecue when one said to the other, "What's a nice **plaice** like you doing in a **grill** like this?"

Barman

A barman looks up in AMAZEMENT as a set of jump leads walks into his pub. "I'll serve you one drink," he says to the jump leads, "but **don't start anything.**"

Beach

Why was the beach disgusted?

The sea weed.

Bear

Which kind of bear is white and you can see right through it?

A POLO BEAR.

Birthday

Which bird flies through the air covered in wrapping paper?

The birthday pheasant.

Bishop

Two Bishops were tucked up in bed.
Which one was wearing a nightie?

Mrs Bishop.

Blue

What's **BLUE** and **SQUARE?**

An  in disguise.

Book

I say, I say why is it
difficult to find a purple library book?

Because they're often taken
to be read!

Boomerang

What do you call a **boomerang** that won't come back?

A stick.

☆☆☆☆☆☆☆☆☆☆☆☆☆☆

Boulder

What did the SHY LITTLE PEBBLE want to be when it grew up?

A little boulder!

☆☆☆☆☆☆☆☆☆☆☆☆☆☆

Boxing

Can a shoe box?

NO, BUT A TIN CAN.

Broomstick

How do you start a broomstick?

There's an **ON/OFF WITCH.**

Butcher

What happened to the butcher's boy who sat on the **bacon** slicer?

He got a *little behind* in his **DELIVERIES!**

BOOM!

BOOM!

Cake

Which cake is vicious and frightening?

Attila the Bun!

Camel

How do you GET DOWN from a CAMEL?

You don't, STUPID!
You get down from a duck!

Cat

**What do you get if you cross a cat
and a duck with a road roller?**

A duck billed flatty puss.

Cheese

Which is the only cheese that is **made** backwards?

EDAMMADE

Chicken

Why did the **chicken** cross the web?

To get to the other site!

Why did the **ELEPHANT** want to cross the road before the **chicken?**

I forget . . .

but the **ELEPHANT** never did!

Why did the **CHICKEN** cross the road?

It was **STUCK** to the elephant's foot like **CHEWING GUM**.

☆

Why did the *chicken* cross the sea?

TO GET TO THE OTHER TIDE!

☆

What goes, Cluck-peck-Cluck-peck-Cluck-peck-**BOOM!**

A *chicken* in a **minefield**.

☆

Chips

A bag of **CHIPS** went into a pub
and the barman said,
"**Sorry**, but WE DON'T SERVE FOOD."

Christmas

The class was talking about Santa Claus in the
run-up to Christmas and teacher asked if anyone
knew how many reindeer pulled Santa's sleigh.
"TWO!" said one small boy.
"Only two?" said teacher. "Are you sure?"
"Sure I'm sure," said the boy.
"It says so in the song :

Rudolph the red nosed reindeer
Had a very shiny nose
And if you ever saw it
You would even say it glowed.
OLIVE, the **OTHER** reindeer..."

Colour

What is the **LOUDEST, rudest, SMELLIEST** colour?

BURPLE!

Computers

What do you call a computer in a raincoat?

MAC.

Cowboy

What is **PINK** but close to **SILVER?**

The Lone Ranger's bum!

Crocodile

A man went into a shoe shop and said to the assistant, "I'm looking for some crocodile shoes." "Certainly, sir," said the assistant. "What size does your CROCODILE take?"

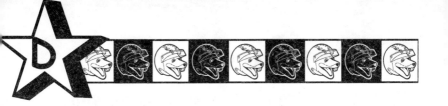

Deer

What do you call a DEER with NO EYES?

No idea
(no eye deer)!

What do you call a DEER with NO EYES and NO LEGS?

Still no idea!

Diarrhoea

What do you give an elephant with diarrhoea?

PLENTY OF ROOM.

Dinosaurs

What do you call a ONE-EYED DINOSAUR?

Dya-thinkee-saurus.

What do you say when you see a ONE-EYED DINOSAUR while walking your dog?

Dya-thinkee-saurus, Rex?

Doctor

The doctor said to his patient, "I'm afraid you are suffering from UPSIDE DOWNINESS." "What do you mean, Doctor?" asked the patient. "Well," said the doctor, "your **nose runs** and your **feet smell**."

"Doctor! Doctor! I keep thinking I'm a belt!" "You can't get **round** me like that, you know."

"Doctor! Doctor!
I keep thinking I'm INVISIBLE."

"I'm afraid I can't see you now."

"Doctor! Doctor!
I still think I'm INVISIBLE!"

"Who said that?"

A man goes to see his doctor with a SANDWICH in his ear, a POT NOODLE on his head, a SAUSAGE up his nose and his face smeared with JAM.
"What do you think is wrong with me, Doctor?" asks the man.

"Obviously," says the doctor, " you haven't been eating properly."

Dolphin

How do dolphins settle an argument?

Flipper coin.

Dracula

Why does DRACULA clean his teeth SIX times a day?

TO AVOID BAT BREATH!

What are DRACULA'S favourite SPORTS?

CASKETBALL AND BATMINTON.

What sort of COFFEE does DRACULA have when he wakes up in the evening?

DECOFFINATED.

Duck

Which side of a duck has the most feathers?

The outside.

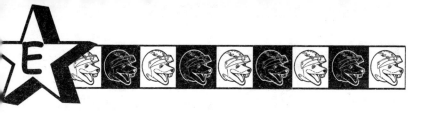

Ears

A man went to the doctor with POTATOES growing in his ears. "This is quite remarkable," said the doctor. "I know!" said the man. "I planted carrots!"

Eggs

Two eggs were frying at breakfast time in the monastery kitchen. "Oh, well," said one egg, "I suppose it's out of the FRYING PAN and into the FRIAR."

Why was the USELESS COOK arrested for cruelty? Because he beat an egg and battered a fish so badly.

Elephant

What do you get when an **elephant** sits on the Batmobile?

Flatman and Ribbon!

★★★★★★★★★★★★★

Why were the four **elephants** kicked out of the swimming pool?

They only had two pairs of trunks between them!

★★★★★★★★★★★★★★

Why are **elephants** BIG and GREY and WRINKLY?

Because if they were SMALL and COLOURFUL and SMOOTH they would be Smarties!

What do you get if you cross an **elephant** with the abominable snowman?

A jumbo yeti!

What's the difference between a SOFT, grey **elephant** and SOFT, grey **paper**?

You can't wipe your bottom with an **elephant**!

Why do **elephants** have TRUNKS?

They really don't suit bikinis.

Eskimo

Whats an ig?

An Eskimo's house with **NO LOO**.

E.T.

Why does **E.T.** have such big eyes?

You would too if you'd seen his phone bill.

Everything

What comes at the **end** of **everything**?

ING. ★

Eyes

There were **2 eyes** and one said to the other,

"Between **you** and **me** something smells!

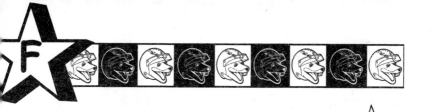

Factory

A whole consignment of **WIGS** was stolen from the **WIG** factory.

Police brushed for prints then combed the area.

Fish

What do you call fish with no eyes?

Fsh.

You would think that fish would be more clever.

After all, they stay in schools forever!

Fleas

How do FLEAS get from one DOG to ANOTHER?

They itch a lift!

How do you start a flea race?

One, two, flea, GO!

Fly

What's the difference between a fly and a bird?

A bird can fly but a fly can't bird.

What has two legs and flies?

A tramp's trousers!

Fluff

What's pink and fluffy?

Pink fluff.

What's blue and fluffy?

Pink fluff holding it's breath.

Football

What do you call a girl in goal?

Annette.

France

Which FRENCH town has TWO TOILETS?

Toulouse.

- - - - - - - -

Frog

"Doctor," said the weak voice on the phone, "I think I'm turning into a frog." "HOLD ON!" said the doctor.

DON'T CROAK BEFORE I GET THERE!

Did you hear about the **frog** whose car got **clamped?**

It was toad away.

Fur

What kind of FUR do you get from a WEREWOLF?

AS FUR AS POSSIBLE!

Gamekeeper

An old gamekeeper was walking round the estate with the lord of the manor. His Lordship was *SURPRISED* and a bit *DISGUSTED* to see the gamekeeper reach over into the cow's field as they walked past, grab a handful of *DUNG* and rub it on his lips.

"WHAT on EARTH did you do that for?" asked his Lordship.

"Got CHAPPED LIPS from this cold weather," said the old gamekeeper.

"And does THAT STUFF heal them?" asked his Lordship.

"Not exactly," said the old man, "but it sure *stops me lickin' em.*"

Gardener

A little boy saw a gardener working on his allotment carrying a huge great *bucketful* of *steaming dung.*

"Phwoa!" said the boy when he caught a sniff of the whiff. **"WHAT** are you going to do with **THAT?"** "Aha," said the gardener, "I'm going to put it on my *strawberries.*"

"Yeeuch!!" yelled the boy. We have ***cream on ours!"***

Ghosts

What do *GHOSTS* have for *PUDDING*?

I scream!

Who is the most important player in the *GHOSTS* football team?

The ghoulkeeper.

Giraffe

What's worse than a **GIRAFFE** with a sore neck?

A millipede with in-growing toenails.

Gnu

What's the difference between a down-and-out, scruffy, smelly gnu and a dead bee?

One is a
SEEDY BEAST
and the other is a
BEE DECEASED.

Two **LIONS** were lazing by a waterhole late one afternoon when some **ANTELOPE** came to drink. The antelope were very nervous when they saw the lions.

"Aren't you going to **ATTACK** us?" asked one of the antelope. "You usually like to eat around now."

"No," yawned one of the lions. "We're waiting for the early evening gnus."

Goats

Two goats found some **rubbish** dumped near their field and started chewing a **video tape**.

"This film's pretty good," said one.

"Yeah, but I preferred the book," was the reply.

God

God **YAWNED** and *stretched*; creating the universe was hard work. "I've just invented a period of **24 HOURS** of **DARKNESS** and light for the world," God said to one of his angels.

"So what are you going to do now?" asked the angel.

"I think I'll call it a day."

Goldfish

The **fish** would have won the cricket match against the **crabs** if they hadn't had the

goldfish bowl.

Gorilla

It was a sad day when the old **gorilla** at the zoo finally died. He was a great attraction; he always made the children laugh and everyone loved him. *UNFORTUNATELY*, the zoo couldn't afford to buy a new gorilla, but the head keeper had a bit of a brainwave. His brother-in-law was an out-of-work actor, so he asked him to dress in a gorilla suit and go in the gorilla's cage.

"No one will know you're not a real **gorilla**," said the head keeper. "No one gets close enough. All you have to do is lark around like the other gorilla did, the children will *laugh* and everyone will love you."

So the actor put on the *gorilla suit* and got in the cage. He *larked around* and made the children *laugh*. Then he *larked around* some more, climbing up the bars of his cage. Everyone loved him. Unfortunately, he *larked around* a bit too much and fell out of his cage into the tiger's cage. The *TIGER* immediately leapt on him.

"HELP!" screamed the actor.
"HELP ME!"

"SHUT UP," said the tiger, "or we'll *BOTH BE SACKED!"*

Grape

What did the *grape* say when it was *squished*?

Nothing, it just gave *a little* wine.

Green

What's *green* and can *kill you* if it falls from a tree and lands on your head?

A snooker table.

Grey

What's GREY and has to be home before MIDNIGHT?

Cinderelephant.

Ha Ha Ha

Hard

What's brown and WHITE and hard?
A hamster with a flick knife.

What's **black** and *white* and **HARD?**

A MATHS TEST.

52 Boomtastic

Head

A **head** sat on a table at a disco, **crying** its eyes out. When somebody asked it why it was so upset, it said:

"I've got no body to dance with!"

Hedgehog

What did the hedgehog say to the cactus?

"Is that you, Mum?"

What do you get if you cross a **hedgehog** with a **road roller?**

A very flat hedgehog!

Hippies

Where can you still find HIPPIES?

At the top of your leggies.

Hole

A policeman came across 3 holes in the ground, scratched his chin for a while and then said:

Well, well, well.

Horse

What sport do **HORSES** like best?

STABLE TENNIS.

What animal has four legs, hooves and stripes all over?

A horse in his pyjamas.

Hospital

Early one morning, two workmen rushed into the casualty department of the **hospital**. One of them was clutching his throat and couldn't speak. "**Somebody help!**" said the workman who could talk. "My mate's got a terrible, sharp pain in his throat!"

"**I'm not surprised,**" said the nurse. "You would too if you had **swallowed** a **pencil** for breakfast."

"What makes you think he'd be so **stupid** as to swallow a pencil?" asked the workman.

"**Easy,**" said the nurse. "**He's got a sausage behind his ear.**"

Hot

What's faster HOT or COLD?

HOT, YOU CAN CATCH COLD.

Hum

What do you get if you cross a bell with a humming bird?

A hum dinger.

Hump

What do you call a **CAMEL** with **3** humps?

Humphrey.

Hunting

A man booked himself on an ADVENTURE HOLIDAY to Canada where he was going to see the GREAT OUTDOORS with the help of an experienced guide. When he got to the REMOTE CAMPSITE, the guide was getting ready to set off into the forest.

"Have you ever hunted bear?" **asked the guide.**

"NO, **said the man,** *"BUT I ONCE WENT FISHING IN SHORTS."*

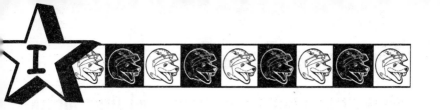

Ice

What goes BLACK-WHITE-BLACK-WHITE-BLACK-WHITE?

A PENGUIN ROLLING DOWN AN ICEBERG.

Idiot

How do you keep an *idiot* in suspense?

I'll tell you tomorrow!

How do you sink an *idiot's* submarine?

Knock on the hatch.

Incredible

What's BIG and green and sits sobbing in the corner?

THE INCREDIBLE SULK.

What's BIG, green, WRINKLY and sobs in the Post Office on Tuesdays?

THE INCREDIBLE SULK'S
GRANNY (ON PENSION DAY).

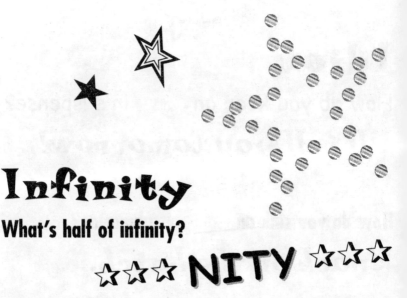

Infinity

What's half of infinity?

✩✩✩ **NITY** ✩✩✩

Inflatable

The inflatable boy got up one morning, said goodbye to his inflatable Mum and Dad and left his inflatable house to go to his inflatable school where he met his inflatable friends and showed them something he had brought to the inflatable school that morning as a joke: **A PIN**. The inflatable boy's inflatable friends were shocked and the inflatable boy was spotted by an inflatable teacher who immediately took the pin from him.

"What are you doing with this?" she yelled at him. "You know pins are against the rules here! Mess around with pins and not only will you let yourself down, you'll let your friends down, you'll let your parents down, you'll let me down and you'll let the whole school down!"

Insect

What do you do if you are _allergic_ to _biting insects._

DON'T BITE ANY!

What do you call a fly with no wings?

A WALK.

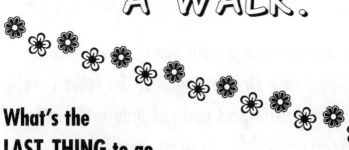

What's the LAST THING to go through an INSECT'S mind when it flies into a car?

Its bum!

Jail

Two **DRUNKS** were on their way home from a fancy dress party dressed as a **MOBILE PHONE** and a **FIREWORK**. They got into an argument and the **MOBILE PHONE** punched the **FIREWORK** just as a police car drove past. The two were arrested and taken to jail.

The next morning

the PHONE WAS CHARGED and the FIREWORK WAS LET OFF.

Jam

Why did the jammy biscuit burst into tears?

BECAUSE ITS MUM HAD BEEN A WAFER SO LONG.

Jelly

What goes **UP** and **DOWN**
and wobbles about?

A jellycopter!

Why should you never go into the **jungle** first thing in the **morning?**

That's when the elephants have their parachute practice.

Why does the duck-billed platypus **have a FLAT FACE?**

It went into the jungle first thing in the morning.

Kangaroo

What do you call a kangaroo
at the North Pole?

Lost!

Keep fit

A man was told by his doctor that to keep himself fit he should walk five miles a day. By the end of the first week he felt much better but he was thirty-five miles away.

King

Why did King Henry VIII have six wives?

He was always chopping and changing.

Knight

What is a knight's favourite food?

SWORDFISH.

Knots

A **ragged** piece of string walked into a police station.

"I'm lost!" wailed the string.

"GOOD HEAVENS!" cried the desk sergeant. "Are you a piece of talking string?"

"No," said the raggedy string, "I'm a frayed knot."

Lake

What do you get if you cross a _lake_ with a _leaky boat_?

About half way and very wet!

Legal

What's the difference between legal and illegal?

One is lawful and the other is a sick bird.

Lemon

What do you give a LEMON that's been cut in half?

✚ LEMON-AID. ✚

What can a whole LEMON do that half a LEMON can't?

Look round.

What do you get if you feed a LEMON to a cat?

A sour Puss.

Letters

What word starts with 'e' and ends with 'e' but only has *one letter* in it?

ENVELOPE!

Lighthouse

What do you call a man with a lighthouse on his head?

CLIFF.

Lion

The LIONS were relaxing in their enclosure at the zoo when the zoo keeper arrived with their lunch.

"WHAT WOULD YOU LIKE TODAY, LEO?" the keeper asked the biggest lion. "ONE STEAK OR TWO?"

"I'll have.......................... ....two," said Leo.

"OKAY", said the keeper.
"But why the BIG PAUSE?"

"Well what do you expect on a lion?" said Leo, lifting his foreleg.

 "HOOVES?"

What do you call a LION without an EYE?

A LON.

✩✩✩✩✩✩✩✩✩✩✩✩✩✩✩✩✩✩✩

TWO LIONS were walking through the **SHOPPING CENTRE.**
One turned to the other and said,

"Bit quiet for a Saturday, isn't it?"

✩✩✩✩✩✩✩✩✩✩✩✩✩✩✩✩✩✩✩

Log

Did you hear about the restless man who wished he could sleep like a log?

HE WOKE UP IN THE FIREPLACE.

Longest

What's the longest word in the world?
Smiles because there's a **MILE**
between the beginning and end!

♥ ♥ ♥ ♥ ♥ ♥ ♥ ♥ ♥ ♥ ♥ ♥

Lorry

Why couldn't the LORRY move A FOOT?

It was only a toe truck!

♥ ♥ ♥ ♥ ♥ ♥ ♥ ♥

Love

**The girl said: "You remind
me of a stormy sea."**
**The boy replied: "You mean because I am
wild, deep and romantic?"**
The girl said: "No, you make me sick."

Lumberjack

A trainee lumberjack went to pick up his equipment from the tool store. The tool store manager gave him a CHAINSAW.

"BE CAREFUL with this," said the manager. "This can cut down SIX trees an hour."

The trainee came back later in the afternoon. "There must be SOMETHING WRONG with this," he said, handing back the CHAINSAW. "It's taken me ALL DAY just to cut down one tree."

The tool store manager picked up the CHAINSAW and PULLED THE CORD to start the motor.

"HEY!" said the trainee.

"WHAT'S THAT NOISE?"

Lunch

What contains TWO EGG SANDWICHES and a KIT-KAT and hangs around FRENCH cathedrals?

The lunch pack of Notre Dame.

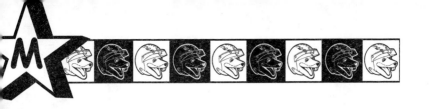

Mechanic

What do you call a mechanic with a
car on his head?

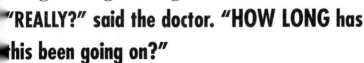

Memory

A MAN went to see his doctor because he had
been having problems remembering things.
"Doctor," said the man, "I keep
forgetting things all the time."
"REALLY?" said the doctor. "HOW LONG has
this been going on?"
"How long has what been going on?" said the
man. "And who are you, anyway?"

Mexican

How do you make a

Mexican chilli?

STICK A FEW ICE CUBES IN HIS SOMBRERO!

Migration

Why do birds fly *SOUTH* for the winter?

Because it's too far to walk!

A WOMAN phoned her doctor one morning and said, "DOCTOR, you have to help me. MY HUSBAND THINKS HE'S A BIRD."

"YOU MUST send him to SEE ME at once," said the doctor.

"I CAN'T," said the woman.

"He's flown south for the winter."

Monster

What do MONSTERS like to have on toast?
BAKED BEINGS.

What does a MONSTER eat after the dentist has polished his teeth?

The dentist.

Two MONSTERS were on their way to school.
"WE HAD BURGLARS LAST NIGHT," said the first MONSTER.
"Really?" said the other. "What were they like?"
"Pretty good," said the first MONSTER, "but teachers taste better!"

Two MONSTERS were eating a clown. One said to the other, "DOES THIS TASTE FUNNY TO YOU?"

Motorbike

What are the funniest motorbikes in the world?
Yamaha-ha-has and Suzuki-hee-hees!

Mount Everest

What do you call a *mini-cab* driver on *Mount Everest?*

LOST!

Mouse

What is small, grey, lives behind the skirting board and sucks your blood?

A mouse-quito!

Mr & Mrs

Mr BIGGER was very BIG. Mrs BIGGER was also very BIG. They also had a baby boy. Which of the three was the biggest?

THE BABY BOY – HE WAS JUST A
LITTLE BIGGER!

Mummy

How can you tell when an EGYPTIAN MUMMY is angry?

HE FLIPS HIS LID!

Musician

Did you hear about the musician who got his head stuck in his piano?

He was trying to play by ear

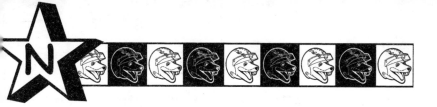

Nelson

Why couldn't **ADMIRAL NELSON'S** men play cards?

He was standing on the deck.

Newsagent

Did you hear about the **stupid** newsagent who opened a **paper shop?**

It blew a w a y !

Nostril

"Aaargh!" yelled the man on the bus.
"A wasp just stung me on the nostril!"
"Which one?" asked another passenger.
"I don't know!" cried the man.

"Wasps all look the same to me!"

Nudist

What **animal** does a nudist look like?

A little bear!

Numbers

Why was six scared of seven?

Because he heard

seven
ate
nine!

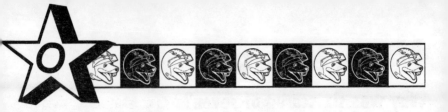

O

What did O say to 8?

Hey, nice belt!

Ocean

What did the ocean say to the beach?

Nothing, it just waved.

What's the best cure for seasickness?

Sit under a tree.

Who is the most powerful villain in the ocean?

The Codfather!

Ogre

What's an ogre's favourite game?

Swallow my leader.

Old

Two OLD DOGS were advertised for sale with the notice:

Buy one, get one flea!

One-armed bandit

Why did the **one-armed bandit** cross the road?

To get to the secondhand shop.

Optician

A man went into an OPTICIAN'S and said, "I keep seeing **BRIGHT** *purple* spots everywhere I look."

"Have you seen a doctor?" asked the optician.

"No, just bright purple spots."

☆☆☆☆☆☆☆☆☆☆☆☆☆☆☆

Orange

Why did the ORANGE take the day off school?

He wasn't peeling well!

The hen sat CLUCKING in the hen house, STRAINING and PUSHING until, finally, to the surprise of all the other hens and her little chick children, she laid **AN ORANGE** instead of an egg!

"Wow!" said one of her chicks.

"Look at the orange Mama laid!"

Ostrich

A truck driver was travelling through a lonely part of AFRICA when his truck broke down. He lifted the bonnet and took a look at the engine but couldn't figure out what had gone wrong. Just then an ostrich with a RED SCARF round his neck came strutting up and stuck his head under the bonnet.

"Aha," said the ostrich. "Your fuel pump has broken. There's a garage in the next town about three miles up the road. They'll fit a new one for you. It should cost about £200."

"Er, thanks," said the startled trucker. "Then he ran all the way to the next town."

"You'll never guess what happened," he gasped as he reached the garage. "My truck broke down and an **ostrich** told me it was the fuel pump and you would fit a new one for £200!"

"Really?" said the garage boss. "Did it have a **RED SCARF** round its neck?"

"Yes!" said the trucker.

"Ignore him," said the garage boss. "He doesn't know a thing about fuel pumps let alone our labour charges!"

Owl

Did you hear about the *l a z y* owl who NEVER WASHED and WOULDN'T TALK?

It stank and didn't give a hoot!

How do we know that
OWLS are smarter than CHICKENS?

Ever heard of
Kentucky Fried Owl?

Why was the owl so quiet when it rained?

BECAUSE HE WAS TOO WET TO WOO!

Pant

What goes, PANT! PANT!

A pair of pants!

Peanut

Two PEANUTS walked into a bar.

One was A SALTED.

Penguin

How do penguins get to school?

By icicle!

Piano

What's the difference between a piano and a fish?

 You can't tuna fish.

★

Pigs

Where do PIGS most like to live?

HAMERICA.

★

Pikachu

How do you get Pikachu on a bus?

Pokemon!

How do you stop PIGS from smelling?

STUFF CORKS IN THEIR NOSES.

Plumber

What do you call a PLUMBER with a *toilet* on his head?

Lou.

What do you call a FEMALE PLUMBER with *two toilets* on her head?

Lulu.

Polar Bear

Why do polar bears have WHITE FUR COATS?

Because they'd look stupid in pink anoraks.

Police

A man ran into a POLICE STATION with his clothes **all torn.**

"Sergeant," he said to the police officer behind the desk, "I've just been **mugged** by a GIANT INSECT who **beat me up** and took ALL MY MONEY."

"YES," said the sergeant, "I heard there was a **nasty bug going around.**"

What's the difference between a **soldier** and a **policeman?**

YOU CAN'T DIP A POLICEMAN IN YOUR EGG!

Pope

What is the POPE'S favourite CHEESE?
Swiss cheese it's the most holey!

Porcupine

What do you get if you cross a GIRAFFE with a porcupine?

A FIVE-METRE-HIGH WALKING TOILET BRUSH.

What sound do **porcupines** make when they kiss?

OUCH!!

Pranks

Which monster likes to play jokes on you?

Prankenstein!

Pudding

Which pudding is fruity and tasty but never stops complaining?

Apple grumble!

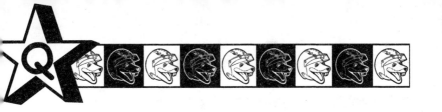

Quack!

"QUACK!" said the duck as it walked into the chemist's shop. "I've got really sore lips."

"OH, DEAR," said the chemist. "TRY SOME OF THIS LIP BALM."

"THANKS," said the duck.

"CAN YOU PUT IT ON MY BILL?"

"QUACK! QUACK!" yelled the duck to his friend as the hunters O P E N E D   F I R E, and his friend yelled back:

"I'm goin' as quack as I can!"

Quad bikes

Why couldn't the *motorbike* join in the **QUAD BIKE** race?

It was just two tyred.

Queen

Why is BRITAIN so WET?

Because the Queen has been reigning for years!

Rabbit

How do you catch a RABBIT?

Hide behind a wall and make a noise like a lettuce.

....

How do you catch a UNIQUE RABBIT?

Unique up on him.

....

How do you catch a TAME RABBIT?

The tame way.

....

How do you catch a NAUGHTY RABBIT?

Naughty tame way.

Race

A cat from Oxford University and a cat from Paris University had a boat race on the Thames. To make things fair, each was rowing the same kind of boat with the same kind of oars and each cat wore the same number. The Oxford cat wore the number ONE-TWO-THREE and the Paris cat wore the French version, Un-Deux-Trois. They started off neck and neck with ONE-TWO-THREE rowing hard and Un-Deux-Trois staying level. Then ONE-TWO-THREE shot into the lead as the Un-Deux-Trois cat sank.

Raisin

Why did the RAISIN ask the **PRUNE** to go to the dance?

Because he couldn't get a date.

Referee

If there is a REFEREE in football and an UMPIRE in cricket, what do you get in *bowls?*

Fruit.

Restaurant

What did the frog order at the restaurant?

French flies and a *diet croak.*

River

What has **five eyes** and **lies on its bed** all day?

The Mississippi River.

Road

A man walks into a pub carrying a **ROLL** of **TARMAC** and says to the barman,

"PINT OF LAGER, PLEASE, and ONE FOR THE ROAD."

What do you call a **workman** named Richard with a road roller on his head?

FLA TRICK.

Rottweiler

A MAN went to see his **DOCTOR** and told him that he had this strange notion that he had turned into a ROTTWEILER DOG.

"I see," said the doctor. "Lie down on the couch, please."

"I CAN'T," said the man. "I'M NOT ALLOWED ON THE FURNITURE."

Rugby

It was a tough rugby match.
One player left the pitch with

- a broken nose,
- a fat lip,
- a torn ear,
- two broken teeth and
- a mangled finger,

*but he hadn't a clue
who they belonged to.*

Rustle

What **rustles** outside your front
door every morning?

A PAPER BOY.

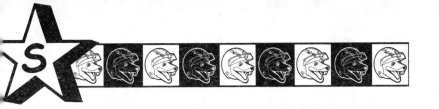

Sandal

What do you call a **FRENCHMAN** wearing **SANDALS**?

Philippe Phlop!

Shrink

A bloke went to see his doctor, sat on the chair in his surgery and said, "**DOCTOR, YOU MUST HELP ME. I'M** SHRINKING!"
"Who said that?" asked the doctor, looking round.
"ME," said the man. "I'M DOWN HERE on the chair."
"OH", said the doctor, looking over his desk at the little man on the chair. "We must try to do something about this but it may take a while, so from now on YOU'LL HAVE TO BE A LITTLE PATIENT."

Silly

Which COUNTRY is most SILLY?

Twitzerland.

Skeletons

Why couldn't the skeleton go sky diving?

HE DIDN'T HAVE THE GUTS.

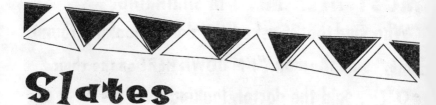

Slates

What do you call a WOMAN with SLATES on her head?

RU TH.

Smell

What's green and smells?

A Hulk fart.

Snake

Which snake acts like a baby?

One with a rattle.

Snowman

What do you call a snowman lying on the beach?

A puddle.

Spooks

Which spook ate all the porridge?

Ghouldilocks.

Spy

What do you call a **wet** and WEEDY spy?

James Pond!

Sticky

What's brown and sticky?

A STICK.

Stink

What has a real stink **and flies?**

A dead skunk.

Suitcase

What's BROWN and HAIRY, wears sunglasses and carries a suitcase?

A coconut going on holiday.

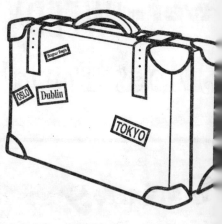

Summer

What wears a long coat and pants in the summer?

A dog.

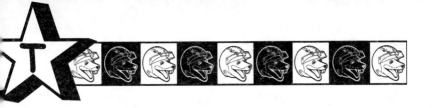

Table

Which knight made King Arthur's table round?

Sir Cumference!

Tail

What makes a PIG'S TAIL like getting up at four in the morning?

It's really twirly.

Tarzan

What did Tarzan say when he saw the elephants by the watering hole?

There are the elephants by the watering hole!

What did Tarzan say when he saw the elephants by the watering hole wearing sunglasses?

Nothing, he didn't recognize them.

Tea

What kind of TEA do FOOTBALLERS DIVE for?

Penal-tea!

Teacher

Why did the ONE-EYED TEACHER have an easy life?

She only had one pupil!

✓

Why are TEACHERS like a box of CHOCOLATES?

Most of them are soft but there are always a few nutty ones.

✓

What's the difference between a **boring teacher** who drones **on** and **on** and **on** and **on** ... and **on** and **on** ... and **on** and a cupboard?

YOU CAN SHUT THE CUPBOARD UP!

Teeth

What's the best thing to put in a pizza?

YOUR TEETH

Tents

What are SMALL, round, GREEN and go camping in tents?

Boy sprouts!

Thermos

David Beckham walks into the England changing room carrying a thermos flask.

"What's that?" asks one of the other players.

"It's a thermos," says David. **"I bought it because they told me it would keep hot things hot and cold things cold."**

"What have you got in it now then?" asks the other player.

"A cup of coffee and a choc ice," says David.

Throw

What sort of meringues can you never throw away?

BOOMERINGUES. *BOOMERINGUES. BOOMERINGUES. BOOMERINGUES.*

Time

A little girl asked her dad what the time was. Her father proudly pulled out the **large, *heavy*, GOLD** pocket watch his grandfather had given him . . . and promptly **DROPPED** it on the floor.

"Oh, dear!" said the girl as her father picked up the watch. "Did your watch stop when it hit the floor, Dad?"

"Of course it did!" said her father.

"Did you think it would go straight through?"

Toad

What do you call a girl sitting in a pond with a toad on her head?

Lily.

Toilet

THIEVES broke into the **POLICE STATION** and stole the *only toilet.*

The police had nothing to go on.

Tree

What do you call a **MEAT-EATING** tree.

Carniferous.

HA Ha Ha Ha

Ugh!

A little boy ran into the kitchen shouting,
"Mum can I lick the bowl?"

"CERTAINLY NOT!" said his mother.

"Just flush it like everyone else."

Underpants

What do you call a boy wearing paper pants?

RUSSELL!

Undertaker

What's the difference between an undertaker and his dog?

The undertaker wears a full morning suit and a top hat but the dog only pants.

Underwater

Where is the best place to sleep underwater?

On the sea bed.

What's pink, lives underwater and carries a machine gun?

Al Caprawn

Underwear

What kind of underwear can do 120**km/h**?

Honda pants!

Urgent

What was so **urgent** that the toilet had to **run** all the way **DOWN** the hill?

It had to get to the bottom fast!

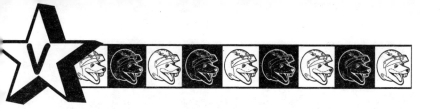

Vampires

Did you hear about the **two** VAMPIRES that ran the marathon?

They finished NECK AND NECK.

What **food** scares VAMPIRES most? Garlic?

NO, BIG STAKES!

How do you know when a
VAMPIRE's got a cold?

There's a
terrible
coffin noise.

What does the **VAMPIRE
POSTMAN** deliver?

Fang mail.

What do you get when a **VAMPIRE**
attacks a *snowman?*

FROSTBITE!

Vanilla

What do you get if you
cross a football team with
an ice cream?

Varnish

How do you get rid of varnish?

Take away the **R** and make it VANISH

Vegetables

What's the difference between SPROUTS and BOGEYS?

Kids hate eating sprouts!

WHO ROCKS the VEGETABLE department in the supermarket?

Elvis Parsley!

How do you MEND A LETTUCE?

With a cabbage patch.

What lives in the VEGETABLE department and ROBS YOU?

Dick Turnip.

What made all the VEGETABLES in the fridge BLUSH?

They saw the salad dressing.

Vest

What did the
POLICEMAN
say to his belly button?

 *You're under a vest!*

Vet

A woman took her pet rabbit to the **vet** because it hadn't been eating properly and didn't seem very well. The **vet** examined the rabbit carefully.

"Ah, yes," said the vet. "He's got a bit of a tummy bug."

The vet took a bottle of medicine from a shelf and handed it to the woman.

"Try to make him take a spoonful of this once a day for the next week and he'll be fine", said the vet. "That will be £25, please."

"TWENTY-FIVE POUNDS?" said the woman. "But you hardly even **looked** at poor Bunny. I expected you to be far more thorough."

"All right," said the vet.

"Nurse! Bring in Rex!"

The nurse brought in a Golden Labrador, who walked up to the rabbit, sniffed it and barked twice, then licked it and barked twice. "Very good," said the vet.

"Now bring in Felix."

The nurse brought in a big black-and-white cat which the vet took and held over the rabbit, moving the cat back and forth. The cat purred.

"Yes, it's definitely only a tummy bug," said the vet. "That will be £125, please."

"But you only asked for £25 BEFORE!" shrieked the woman.

"I know," said the vet, "but now you've had the lab tests and the cat scan!"

Virus

Why did the computer go to the doctor?

He had some kind of virus.

Vulture

Two VULTURES were sitting in a tree having just eaten an UNFORTUNATE TRAVELLER who had died way out in the desert.

"I feel sick," **said the first vulture.**

"Me too," **said the other.** *"You just can't keep a good man down."*

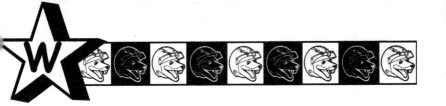

Warden

Why do TRAFFIC WARDENS have yellow bands around THEIR HATS?

To stop people parking on their heads.

Warren

What do you call a boy with **6 RABBITS** down his trousers?

Warren.

Week

How many *days of the week* begin with **T**.

All of them, MILK and 2 sugars, please!

Whales

Why do WHALES only swim in SALT WATER?

Because pepper water makes them s n e e z e !

How do **WHALES** check their weight?

They go to a whale way station.

Window

A shop WINDOW had been smashed by a falling tree in a storm. The shop owner called in a specialist company to remove the old broken WINDOW and install a new one. The shopkeeper watched as one workman hacked the broken pieces out of the WINDOW frame. The workman stuck his head in through the broken WINDOW. "Any chance of a cup of tea?" he called. Just then a large piece of glass fell from the top of the WINDOW frame and chopped off the workman's ear.

"**AAARRGH!**" screamed the workman. "That glass just ***chopped off*** me EAR!" The shopkeeper spotted an ear lying on the floor. "IS THIS IT?" he asked, anxious to help.

"**NAW,**" said the workman.

"Mine had a pencil behind it!"

Witches

What kind of tests do student WITCHES do?

Hex-ams!

How do you make a WITCH wriggle?

Give her T to make her TWITCH!

How do you make a WITCH scratch?

Take away w to make her ITCH!

What do **COOL** WITCHES ride?

Vrrrrroooom sticks!

Did you hear
about the witch who had a
husband and ATE KIDS?

What does
a WITCH use to
correct her magic?

A SPELL CHECKER.

Wood

Did you hear about the **wooden car** with **wooden seats, wooden bodywork, wooden wheels** and a **wooden engine?**

WOODEN GO!

Woodpecker

What do you call a **WOODPECKER** with **NO BEAK?**

A headbanger!

Workmen

What do you call a **WORKMAN WITH A SPADE** on his head?

Doug.

What do you call a **WORKMAN WITHOUT A SPADE** on his head?

Dougless

Wrong

What word is ALWAYS pronounced wrong?

-Wrong-

X-ray

Why can you NEVER FOOL anyone wearing X-RAY glasses?

THEY CAN SEE RIGHT THROUGH YOU!

Yahoo!

Were only going to do a HALF a day this MORNING . . . announced the teacher.

YAHOOO!! cheered all the pupils.

. . . and we'll do the OTHER HALF day this AFTERNOON.

Year

How many seconds in a year?

Twelve -
January 2nd,
February 2nd,
March 2nd,
. . . .

Yellow

What's *gooey* and YELLOW and smells like banana?

Monkey sick.

**What goes,
THINK YELLOW - BE YELLOW.
THINK YELLOW - BE YELLOW.
THINK YELLOW - BE YELLOW?**

An orange with a part time job as a lemon.

What's YELLOW and lurks in a BISCUIT THEN wakes you up at night with a terrible wailing?

Custard screams!

Yeti

What do you call a YETI in a phone box?

Stuck!

How many WET YETIS do you need to stink out a room?

A phew!

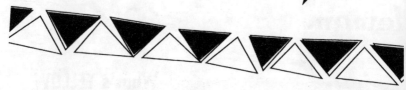

What are a YETI'S favourite days to eat?

Chews-day and Fry-day!

What do you get a YETI for Christmas?

No idea,
but you better
hope he likes it!

Y-fronts

What do you call A BOY with an **encyclopedia** in his **y-fronts?**

Smarty pants!

What do you call A BOY with lots of LITTLE COLOURED SWEETS in his **y-fronts?**

Smartie pants!

What do you call A BOY who has been wearing the same **y-fronts** for **two months?**

DISGUSTING!

Zebra

What looks like HALF a ZEBRA?

⭐ The other half!

//////

What has RED and GREEN stripes and a PURPLE HAT?

A zebra with bad taste.

//////

Where did the ZEBRA get his PURPLE HAT?

At a jungle sale.

//////